# KAN ZAMAN

## JUDITH MANSOUR

*A Memoir in Poetry and Prose*

ISBN 979-8-88596-994-9.

**KAN ZAMAN** – Arabic; (descriptive).
A long time ago. Common usage – once upon a time, during the
golden age, way back when; *colloquial*: and that's how it was.

*Marie Haddad circa 1937*

*For the Three Little Pigs*

# Contents

# Foreword

Between life and loss, there's food. Lots of it. If you're lucky (and I am), you have a friend like Judith who makes it her business to nourish you when you need it. Food is often what connects us: to our friends and relatives, to our ancestors and descendants. It is the eternal symbol of moving forward, being present in the tasks of tending to the needs at hand, to the business of living and loving.

In her essays and poems, Judith tells you the truth. Sometimes it's delightful and naughty and sometimes it's difficult to hear. Truth is in the ingredients. There is cruelty and there is tenderness and sometimes the line between is blurry. Memories of a pat of butter oozing over a little triangular lamb meat pie butts up against the harsh reality of singeing the fleece from the lamb's lifeless body with the kind of blow torch one uses to crust creme brûlée.

The food that comes forth from Judith's hands and heart is the result of recipes deeply buried in her DNA. Throughout her essays and poems, she reveals the cast of characters at whose knees she honed her cooking skills. Her difficult grandfather, Nasif, helps eight-year-old Judith cradle the denuded lamb head as he teaches her how to slice away the ear. She's a failure. Her gentle grandmother, Victoria, on the other hand, protects her and nourishes her after school with m'heeye, a barley lamb mush, a soupy blend of wheat pearls, lamb and chicken bones. The m'heeye itself is a paradox: smelling dreadful while cooking and once ladled into the bowl tasting delicious.

Judith takes us on the journey with Victoria and Nasif when they departed Lebanon. Victoria, who was fourteen at the time, left her family, her life and her dreams behind to fulfill someone else's plans for her to become a wife and an American. She brought with her some food and reserved a loaf of bread as insurance against starvation. It is that petrified loaf of bread that would become the most treasured and fought over heirloom of the Mansour clan. The thing about time is it's so damn finite. Yet what we consume and how we prepare it is carried from one generation to the next as perhaps the most elemental aspect of our human lives. In Judith's *Kan Zaman*, food is transcendent.

Lori Wald

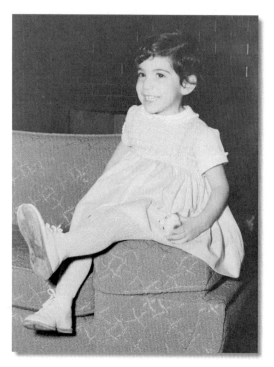

*Judith, age two.*

## Message from the Author

These poems, essays, and stories are memories, faded from sunlight, yellowed with age, wrinkled from sitting in the back of a drawer. Some are not old, but aged me instead, and my memory failed. I've filled in the blanks here and there. Time is tricky when diluted with nostalgia, grief, and longing. So, I might not have it quite right, exactly the way it happened. Oh well, in my mind, that's how it was.

Mu'asafu, kan zaman.

# REDOLENT SUMMER

That smell, you know the one
Damp wooden clothespins holding wet sheets
That stutter and flap
Pulled by the wind
Hot rubber streamers, that hung from your bike
That baked in the sun
While you ate your lunch

Then on bad days,
You know, how the blacktop smelled
Like metal and dirt and cement and must
Just before rain
And your mom called you in
Where a tv tray and couch cover shroud
Made for a fort
Stinking of mothballs
A makeshift tree house or club or tent
'Til the rain stopped and you begged to go out

Come on, you remember don't you?
That smell
That whiff of bacon when Mrs. Elam opened her door
Of Orange Stripe and Juicy Fruit and Grape Bubble Yum
As you sat on the front porch reading your cousin's
Mad Magazine, the one you swiped when he wasn't looking
I know you know it
We both do

It smelled like rust
On the side of that Cutlass
That pulled up the drive weekend mornings
Honking for your sister
Who smelled like Breck and Windsong and hope
Teenage fun
You couldn't wait to have
At BBF after teaching the deaf
Saturday mornings all summer long
To see that guy
That one guy, the one she liked
That just wouldn't ask her out

Don't say you don't remember
That smell that we smelled
The plastic of dollies, petroleum spun bunnies
With Styrofoam pebbles for stuffing inside
Sold at Consolidated, a fraction of the price
That Strouss and McKelvey could charge to the rest
The smell of caps, shot off just for sound
For something to do
As the days stretched ahead
Like hope and butterflies
As you flew from the swing
That you pumped just so high
To make yourself scared

## YELLOW TRANSISTOR

Sly begins to wrastle, a tinny sounding funk
Plucked over the airwaves
And onto the porch
A pyramid of sandwiches, a brown Melmac base
Salted tomatoes and Schwebel's soft white
Head lettuce, Spin Blend, bologna, pickle loaf
Just one slice
Barely a sandwich, to make it go farther
So many mouths, only one salary
Kool-Aid sangria in tall blue tumblers
Of ice cold aluminum that hurt your teeth
Sweet, chunky gulps, drunk with abandon
Washed down hopscotch, Double Dutch,
And ruthless games of tag
Troyer Farms chips
Slipped between the slices, a crunchy condiment
For texture and taste
Sly is grateful to be himself all over again
Boots Bell spins Three Dog Night,
Who croon, mourn
How can people be so heartless?
From the yellow transistor
That hangs from Mom's wrist

## THE COMPOUND

I close my eyes
To worry a dream
A door creaks open on Michigan Avenue
Sitthie stands at the kitchen sink
A braid down her back
Coffee and cookies
Smells of love
Ice cream with whipped cream, chewy candies gone hard
Jid's brown bag
Delivered like gold
Grape leaves, dandelions, neck bones from Hughes
He flips a Schlitz, pours salt down the neck
A "swink", a sigh, a burp
Sour balls, Basra, and Gubbermen' Club
Shots for the boys
Red licorice for the girls

At Fifth and Park
Aunt Clara's apartment
White Monte Carlo with blue Landau roof
China and crystal
Pretty things to touch
A big mink coat to model for fun
Jiffy Pop popcorn
Scary movies and sleepovers
Painting our nails, our lips, our faces
With bright red lipstick
In the bathroom mirror

Hold my hand
Let's cross the street
Uncle George and Aunt Connie
The couple confetti
Bourbon and ginger
Pizza and poker

Parties and people
All hours of the day
Pipe smoke
A hug that clung to my hair
The cousins, all older and cooler and wild
Hendrix, the Beatles, the Byrds, the Stones
George Jr. in Hair
On Broadway, the Met
Jesus Christ Superstar, such a great role
Dropped from his rickshaw
Pilate's punishment
Millennia too late

Caddy-corner families
Across the compound called us
Come on home
Make Room for Daddy
Let's build St. Jude
A shrine for our people
To pray for sick kids
In the dawn of life
Daddy's passion, pervasive for all
Mama was music
The opera and choir
Symphony concerts
Dinners at midnight

The boys were cars
Albums and tennis
Washing and waxing to
Earth, Wind, & Fire
The girls were clogs
Purses and sewing
Blender made milkshakes
When mom wasn't home
Aunts for scoldings
Uncles for jokes

We were a tribe, a pack, a kill
Until Death, a dodge ball
Ruthless and cruel
Started a game
Picking us off
One by one

# PROMISED

Nasif Dukhlallah Mansour Bou Noffil and Victoria Loobis Simaan boarded the SS Constitution in April 1917 and came to the United States from Marjayoun, Lebanon. Their one passport and the ship's manifest listed them as Nasik and Vectoria Mansour, siblings. My grandparents were not brother and sister. But they were also not yet married. He was 19 and she was 14. Their sponsors would meet them at Ellis Island in New York and accompany them to New Castle, Pennsylvania, where they would settle for a year or two before moving to Youngstown, Ohio permanently.

When Victoria and Nasif boarded the S.S. Constitution, they had the clothes they were wearing and a leather satchel that contained their papers. Nasif wore their money around his neck, wrapped in a dirty rag. They also brought bread, cheese, dried meat, nuts, and dried fruit for the trip. They rode steerage. My sitthie (grandmother) was careful to reserve a loaf of bread – insurance that they would not starve upon arrival. That loaf of bread and its rightful ownership after my grandparents died, sparked the ugliest of fights between the surviving Mansour siblings.

Before the trip, before the plans to emigrate, my great, great aunt began to sew a pale green dress with lace, beads, and intricate stitching. My grandmother, only 12 years old, watched and sometimes helped as her aunt and mother sewed and stitched. Later, my grandmother would learn to look at clothes in department store windows, sketch and replicate them for her daughters.

Victoria had met Nasif when she was 5 or six years old. He had sponsors in America, and a map of her future was set to course. One June day in 1917, Victoria donned the pale green dress, a new pair of shoes, which were not to be worn outside of the house, and sat waiting for the arrival of Nasif and his sisters, Zaineh and Hunnah.

Nasif, Zaineh, and Hunnah arrived at Victoria's home in late afternoon. No one spoke about Nasif and Victoria getting married. No plans for the trip to America were discussed. They talked about the weather. My great grandparents, along with Nasif, his sisters, and Victoria passed an afternoon exchanging pleasantries. They sat adjacent to each other, drank their tea, ate olives, dates, and cheese, and in early evening, before the meal was served, my great grand mother told Nasif and Victoria to go for a walk. Zaineh and Hunnah would accompany them.

Once outside the house and walking up the path, Victoria looked up at Nasif. He caught her eye, and she smiled. He raised his arm, knocked her down, and pushed into a ditch. He called her dog, spit at her, and continued the walk with his sisters. Victoria waited.

On the way back they didn't stop. They didn't help her to stand. She raised herself up and followed them to the house.

In the kitchen with her mother and aunt, Victoria cleaned off the dress as best she could, and wrapped an apron around her to cover the ripped beaded silk. She and her mother did not commiserate. My great grandmother offered Victoria no words of comfort or sympathy. They silently filled platters of food to serve the meal.

My great grandparents, along with several other great, great aunts and uncles and cousins gathered for a meal that included meat that June evening. They ate and drank tea and had dessert and never once discussed a marriage between Nasif and Victoria. The evening ended with game of Basra, cigarettes, and coffee outside for the men. The women sat in the heat of the kitchen and no more was said. It was understood that Victoria was now engaged and would be married upon her arrival in the US in November that same year.

After eight of her nine children were born, Dr. Fisher explained that the pain Victoria always felt in her chest and sides, especially during labor or when she had a cold or cough, was the result of broken ribs that had not healed properly.

# DAD'S DERBUKKE

Hizzy ya hiz
Dad would call
His hands in motion
One slack
One stiff
Beat out a riff
That rises and falls
Like hips making love

Arms at their sides
Hands held tight
The dancers one coil
Weaving, thumping
The lead of the line
Dances in wait
Swivels and shimmies
Into the lair, into the heat

A cacophony of motion
Sex and steps and kicks and sound

A handkerchief, knotted
Swirls like smoke
As hands unhook
Bodies grow close
Dad calls to the beat
Hai-huh, hai-huh
Charming the snake

Incense and sage
Surround the lovers
Who pirouette, sway
A siren song, secret seduction
All from the heat of
Dad's derbukke

## UNDER THE TABLE

Apparently, she was drunk at the funeral. Had a bottle and kept making excuses to go get something out of her car.

Intent on making an anthill of salt and pepper, fingers as makeshift excavator, I focused solely on the tiny white cubes and black and gray dust, shifting them back and forth across the Formica.

Hair tucked under the cotton tharboosh, two of them kneaded and portioned out dough, while the other two pinched balls of seasoned, chopped lamb from a porcelain basin, and pressed it into the discs of dough. Folded on three sides and sealed in the center with butter, it made a triangle.

She always came back empty handed, though.

Everyone knew it was a ruse. She'd resume her place in the receiving line, teetering into the sprays of flowers and giant plants.

Mama brushed butter on the tops of the little triangles, placed them on the baking sheet, and slid them into the oven. When she made these at home, she would bake them until they were done, but then put them under the broiler for just a few seconds, never taking her eyes off of them. A moment too long, and that was that. Ashes.

My aunt reverted to speaking in Arabic if I looked up from my construction site, hearing a bad word or sensing something that was said only with eyes. "Bint," with a flat T sound, means girl in Arabic. So every time I heard that word, I knew they knew I was listening. Then quiet.

Sometimes I'd crawl under the table and create a ruckus, pretending to play at something, so that Mama would tell me to stop and come sit down at the table where she could watch me. Open invitation back to the conversation.

Whoever she was that was drunk at the funeral had no business standing in the line with the family. After all, they were divorced. His mother hated her from the beginning so in a way, she was asking for it by pretending to be the sad widow. His mother cussed her out and called her a sharmuta.

I knew what that meant, but back then, I'd have gotten hot peppers in my mouth for saying so.

My cousin is getting married. They have to make at least 500 of the miniature meat pies — figure two per person, but then of course, some people will act like they've never seen food before, so maybe 600 is a better way to go. Definitely 600.

Mama pulls the cookie sheets from the oven. Juice from the meat pies sluices, sizzling across the pan as Mama, with one short shake, slides them onto a cooling rack. I don't understand how she doesn't burn her fingers. She brushes them again with butter, but not too much. Otherwise they'll go soft.

They agree. If left alone, she'll definitely cause a scene at the wedding. Mama says that Baba told her not worry, he'll keep her
in hand.

They all start laughing. Even Mama.

# BROKEN GLASS

From broken glass
He built a mosaic
Opulent shards, carefully placed
A son! A son!
The diamond crest
That shimmered and glinted
In early morning, before he awoke
By noon, he was coal
From scoldings and don'ts
Then a daughter, an emerald
A most precious jewel
Twirled high in the air
Placed oh so soft in just the right square
Hard to contain
Bled outside the lines
Til nothing was left
Then a few more more
Wrapped in their blankets of lapis and gold
Pieces of pieces, that shone with hope
All contained in platinum barbed wire
Grouted together, bonded by fear
A stained glass window
A rose-colored family

# FAST FORWARD

A pleated skirt
With Peter Pan collar
Ann Frank's Diary across my face
They had years and jeans, eye shadow, platforms
Dances and bell bottoms,
Albums that skipped on their favorite song
Played too often to remember that boy
That kiss, that note, passed in the hall
Discos and strobe lights
I'd never see
And moves never danced beyond my chair
I sat with my Jiddie
Filching his smokes, sipping Sanka
With Cinnamon toast
Playing Basra
And watching Dallas for who shot JR
Then came engagements
And platinum rings
Wealth earned in trade
From an era long gone
Jewelry for flour, coffee, rice
When it was my turn
In marshmallow crème
White slippers and lace
So many were gone
So many more to go
But I couldn't fathom
A world so small
No din, no bustle
No presents to wrap

The ma'amool, the kibbee
The dubke and uud
The mizhwehs, the duff
The pillow for koobez
Traditions are waiting
To be resurrected
By the new generation
That we never had

# M'HEEYE

It's January 19, 1979 at about 3pm. I am 11 years old. My grandmother will die later that night just before 4am.

I don't want to go home. My father has been quietly seething for weeks. My sister has done the unthinkable. She has moved away with her boyfriend. After weeks of forbidding, threatening, yelling, Dad is now silent, which is even worse. My mom has shut down. She sits, stares at her book, but never turns the page.

I step off the school bus into the wet, jagged air. It's just as easy to go home or to Sitthie's – my grandmother Victoria's house. I hold my breath against the cold until I pull at the screen door and then push at the storm door. The smell of stewing lamb bones makes my eyes water.

I kick my snow boots into the basement, and shrug my coat onto the nearest chair. Sitthie's hug smells like skin and olive oil and Ivory soap. I shiver and settle in for a hug. "You're so cold!" she says into my hair. I wrap my arms around her thick waist, and tuck my hands between her apron and housedress. She's soft and round. And warm. She always tickles my neck. I brace for the onslaught, but today she doesn't. She rubs and rubs to calm my shivering.

She's making m'heeye: wheat pearls stewed on lamb and chicken bones and broth. Everyone is always surprised that this stew is so delicious because the smell of the simmering bones is dreadful. Sitthie shuffles to the cupboard, pulls out a serving-size bowl and sets it on the table. It won't be possible for me to consume all of the m'heeye destined for that bowl, and yet she gives me a child's spoon.

I take advantage of being "the baby." I am the youngest girl of the grandchildren, but because the only cousin a few months younger is a boy, he automatically has more privileges. So I'm the baby. My sisters are less than charmed by my ambivalence over whether to play with Barbie Dolls or listen to the Clash. Sitthie doesn't care.

The m'heeye steams in the bowl. Sitthie drops a pat of butter on top. M'heeye is the consistency of oatmeal with shreds of lamb and chicken. It's beige and thick and ugly, not even sprigs of parsley or mint can make it inviting. Salty yellow rivers form as the butter melts on the surface.

Sitthie never eats with me, never slows. She is always sweeping the floor, reheating perked coffee in the stovetop Farberware, dicing onions, or washing dishes. But I never feel ignored. Or in the way. I'm not the pain in the ass my sisters are constantly calling me. I'm Sweetheart, ya roohie, or ya binthie my little girl.

Sitthie has congestive heart failure, so while I stare at the m'heeye, waiting for it to cool, and she asks how are mama and baba, "good" is the answer. The rule, no matter what. I don't look up. She strokes my hair, goes to the Frigidaire to get something for me to drink. Sitthie is diabetic, so Fresca is the only soda she keeps in the house. "I din give you too much, sweetheart. It's no good for you." She knows the rule and doesn't force me to break it by telling her things unpleasant. She pours Fresca into a juice glass with oranges painted on it.

Sitthie disappears into the basement, and I pour more than half of the m'heeye back into the pot, so that as she comes back upstairs, I am spooning the last of it into my mouth. She delights in the fact that I have eaten it all. "Tha'ah" she calls, waving me to the living room. We watch General Hospital because I'm not allowed at home.

At 4:00pm I get up to leave and think, what excuse can I make to stay longer? I pull on my boots and coat, she pinches and tickles my neck. Although I have hugged and kissed my grandmother scores of times, today is the only day I can remember her pulling me into her. Making me linger long enough for my coat to smell like her. She opens the front door and steps out on the porch, and January hits us like broken glass.

I tell her to go back into the house, that it's too cold, but she stays, waving as I cross the street, turn onto Madison, and walk toward Fifth. When I turn around, she is still standing there watching me. When I get home, my mother takes my coat and says, "You smell like your Sitthie."

I try to smile. To coax some emotion from my mom, but tears won't let me.

"What did she feed you?"

"M'heeye." I call as I head up the stairs.

# JID

Eyes, gouged free, stared blankly at the washer, dryer, ceiling, and door. Ears severed clean, lay on a plate. Jid had lined eight lambs' heads and their wrested parts on the sink board in the basement and began to prep them for cooking. The fleece crackled as he lit match after match to singe it away, and after burning through an entire box of matches, he headed to the garage in search of a blowtorch. He returned with a small one, like the one Elton Brown uses to caramelize crème brulee.

The stench of burnt flesh, fleece, and bleach wafted out the door and into the driveway. It stayed in my clothes and then in my nostrils. I sat in the stairwell, revolted, riveted. I was 8 years old, and my grandfather was a tremendous source of curiosity for me: the foods he ate, the stoic demeanor, the fact that he refused to speak English.

Jid carved away all the recognizable features and reserved the flesh in the upturned lid of the white porcelain pot simmering on the stove. He made a broth of eyes, ears, and noses, simmered with celery, onions, bay leaves, and carrots. Jid rinsed dung from stomach linings, pouring the waste down the commode that he then doused with bleach. I knew that the lamb and rice that we were having for dinner would be stuffed into the stomach lining and baked with chicken pieces and brains, and stewed on that broth. Jid always saved the brains for himself. And my dad or Aunt Clara if they happened to stop by.

Tha'a ya bintie (come, little one). I stood from the landing and walked into the basement. I had been watching as Jid carved one entire lamb, and then dissembled and cleaned a bunch of lambs' heads and stomach linings.

He cradled one of the heads in the fold of my arm, positioned a small paring knife in my other hand and guided it to slice away the ear that had just been singed clean. I gagged as the knife pierced cartilage. A hot sticky hand pushed the back of my head, "Hamarra." He grumbled. I knew that meant jackass. My hair got stuck where he'd touched it. Jid took the head from my arm, leaving a trail of goo on my sleeve, and pushed me toward the stairs. I returned to the top step, gagging again and again, bile thick in my throat and nostrils.

## SLICK

Playah, the word
Girls now say
His rooftop was t-topped
Chrome mag wheels and a hood that shone
Self-installed stereo
For the beat to blare and
Bounce off of the seat
Smooth as skin unseen by sun

A set stage
Monte Carlo Coupe, black and gray
Come what may
Girlfriend, lady friend, just need a ride
Front seat fine, bucket seat leaned
Just enough
For that kiss to hold
But whose hand it was, we never did know.
The Limelighter called, Ambrosia on stage
The Theatrical, sly, smokey and jazzed

Then there was Beachcomber, not his scene
No funk, no blues, no rhythm in sight
Bellbottomed bozos and shirts too tight
Top 40 bullshitters who thought they could groove
We knew the name, but not the scene
Orange Room's back room,
Another place to hide
Gabe's was a shithole with watery booze
Girls not his style, all silk and flash
Names left outside
When he rolled in at dawn
To crash on the couch
He was clean, smelled like spice
So said Cardin, designer du jour

His shoes, his jeans, his cologne por homme
A Scotch on the rocks, Teddy Pendergrass blues
When Somebody Knocked,
And they always knocked
Wanting to see who was inside
We met one or two
That we'd spy if we hid
Not dates, he'd snarl
Even when asked, he wouldn't say
Got taken, got took
So now he was slick
Like the guy in the Band
Average White variety
He learned his lesson
Just like the song,
It is after all
Nothing more than a
Schoolboy Crush

# HONOR AND OBEY

He loved her.

He wanted marriage, children, and a life in America.

She wanted poverty, silence, and service in Mary's name. She wanted to be a nun.

Nasif knew from his early teens that Victoria would make a good wife, so it never occurred to him to think of anyone else. She was beautiful, was a loving and dutiful daughter, and she had had some education – seventh grade. He knew her to be a quiet and sweet-tempered girl, so when she was of marriageable age, he asked her parents for her hand. Nasif was offering life in America.

Victoria had always wanted to be a nun. From the time she was a small child, she had the desire to devote her life to the Blessed Mother and to live a quiet life of prayer and service to the poor or sick. A life of silence. Her parents, sister, and brother knew that this was what she wanted. But an offer of life in America would surely trump a life of poverty and hardship.

Wouldn't it?

Victoria's future was decided for her. She prayed to the Blessed Mother to give her strength. She was innocent. And scared. She never had any particular wish to leave her parents, whom she never saw again once they sailed for America. She hoped that by making her wish to become a nun known to Nasif, that he would back away from making the arrangement. Surely, he wouldn't get in the way of a spiritual life.

Nasif did not like that she had to pray for strength to have him as her husband. He did not like that Victoria didn't feel lucky to have the chance for life in America, and he particularly did not like that she thought him an insufferable brute.

Nasif and Victoria never discussed this. Nor did their families or parents.

She did not love him and did not want to marry him. He wanted to marry her and he did love her. He believed she would make a good wife and mother, and therefore, proceeded as planned.

They emigrated through Ellis Island and settled first in New Castle, Pennsylvania, where their sponsors lived. Two months later, the wedding took place. Nasif, Victoria, and their witnesses were the only people present. It was not a festive occasion, nor was it a drab occasion. It was a legal occasion – a civil ceremony, subsequently blessed by Fr. Maroon Eid.

Nasif opened a small dry-cleaning shop. Victoria learned about the duties of a wife. She was to keep the house, cook the meals, and go to church on Sundays. Victoria also helped with Nasif's dry-cleaning shop by taking in laundry and sewing. She even found that she could still devote part of her life to Mary without it interfering with her duties as a wife or mother. Instead, she passed it on to her children as best she could.

Victoria also learned that when her husband wanted sex, it was her duty to provide it. Or at least not fight it. She often said to us, her granddaughters, "Sex is the dirty part of marriage, but if you can stay pregnant, they can't touch you."

# FULL HOUSE

Mama was the mortar
Who held us together
Her limelight, the kitchen
Hands never still
Dishes to scrape,
Crumbs to be swept, hair in someone's eyes
A din in each room
She silently stood
At the sink, at the stove
A quick kiss hello as each guest arrived

Handed off to Dad
To pour a high-ball –stiff
And tell tall tales
Of second story guys, bookies, and cops
Dancing, the Elm's Ballroom
When men wore suits
And hats just because
Stories of movie stars,
Millionaires for the cause
A place for our people
To shine their light

Mom stirred paste into the lamb,
Only one sip
Of a drink fast diluted
By ice, like dreams
That stood no chance
In the heat of her kitchen
M'humsa bubbled with pine nuts of gold
Coaxed into crispness, browned in butter

We flocked to the table
Like moths to the flame
As she mixed the crown jewel
Kibbee nyeh

Grab the green onion
Garnish the plate
Check this for salt
Herbs in harmony
But mint, the soprano
The diva divine
Deepened the flavor while cleansing the tongue

The table grew quiet as mouths grew full
A table of 12 grew up to 40
Sisters and cousins and in-laws and friends
Boyfriends and girlfriends, a friend of a friend
Once invited, they always came back

As bellies got full
Minds would empty
From mouths grown brave
With Arak and wine
Mass is not God
That priest is a joke
This one got married, a gambler, a cheat
She had problems with nerves and booze

Mom rose from her chair, unseen, unheard
Back to the kitchen
Her private terrain
Her stories were told
Through flour and yeast
Rosewater, mint
A pinch of salt to mellow the coffee
Stories through spices and flavors we loved
Mama, the mortar
Who held us together

# BEDTIME STORY

Stay awhile
Just a quick stop
Too long is too long and
It will hurt when you go
Stay so I feel you
Know that you're there
Like when you read stories
From the edge of my bed
The book was perched between your hands
You read, you waited
As I drifted to sleep
Regular breaths
Came in time

Once you were gone
I'd lie awake nights,
Picture your skin
Your nails, your hands
Selecting a book
To read til I slept
I prayed you'd come
And stay for a while

Watch me sleep
I'll know you're there
Pull the covers
Over my shoulder

I yank at the dream
Pull it over my head
I know that you're gone
And you won't be back.

## JUST SOCKS

Her family a drawer of mismatched socks
A half- this here, a step- that there
No two blues were quite alike
But worn under pants
No one could see
She spent her childhood angry, miffed
Where do they go
They can't just vanish
Vowing, she pledged, nothing but mates
Only real pairs when I have all my own
And when she grew up
Nothing but mates
Perfect, pristine
Committed reality in photos and cards
Beautiful, perfect, designer designed
Folded not balled
In the drawer that she saved
She lay them in rows, gradient rows
By color, by length, and use
They just sat
Once worn, they were washed
And from wash they would fade
From wear and tear and love too much
Some got holes as socks are wont
Some went where they go when they never come back
Some made her itch and got cast aside
And once again
Her drawer was awry
All she wanted were clean, matching socks
A family, perfect and rolled in their space
But laundry and wear eventually won
Just like before when she hated them all

# ALLAH YERHAMA (MAY GOD REST HER SOUL)

Nasif leaned into Victoria's casket, crying, stroking her hair. "Habib'et ulbeh; ya eyouni; tha'a ya habibte." Calling his love, his eyes, his heart to please wake up. I had never seen him touch her.

Nasif, his nine children, their spouses, and the scores of grandchildren packed into the room at Shriver Allison Funeral Home. Black veiled women stood pulling their hair, striking themselves in the face, and wailing beside her casket.

A line of condolence callers snaked through the lobby, into the parking lot, with the stabbing cold and snow. They never stopped coming.

The afternoon break, from 4-7pm never happened. It was now after 9:00pm. Nasif's daughters tried to cajole him away from the casket. He pushed them off. All of the friends, and the wailing women in black had gone home, but the family remained. And the priests. They sat in chairs, smoking, and watching Nasif chant Aramaic poetry that no one understood.

My mother had had her coat on for some time. I wanted to go home. Mom stared at Nasif, watching him weep. She shook her head. "He never had a kind word for her and now he mourns …like they were … I don't know." There were tears in her eyes but she didn't cry. She shrugged off her coat and told my brothers to drive my sisters and me home. We lived just around the corner, but during the day, nearly a foot of snow had fallen.

The funeral home was next door to my grandparents' house, separated by a large parking lot. The funeral home was the center of much childhood curiosity with its ambulance drop-offs, casket filled hearses, and people dressed in black. Because our grandparents' house was a second home for all of us grandchildren, that funeral home remains a landmark in our childhoods. We rode our bikes, played tag, hopscotch, and kickball in the parking lot. Now, we were inside.

Nasif grew quieter but stronger the more his children tried to pry him away. Minutes before, I had been itching to go. Suddenly, I did not want to. How could we leave him?

Nearing 10 pm, Uncle George, the oldest son, took my grandfather by the arm. "Come on, Pop." It was a command. Nasif stood from the kneeler, leaned over his wife, looked at her very intently, and shook his head, "Alla yerhama." My father draped a coat over his shoulders. Uncle George took one arm, dad took the other, and my other two uncles followed right behind. They walked him, whimpering, across the parking lot and into his home.

My Aunt Sandra, who still lived at home, told us that until it was time for Nasif to bathe and shave and ready himself for the funeral the following morning, he stayed in his chair all night, coat still over his shoulders, clutching a pillow to his belly, crying.

# SOMEWHERE ELSE

You are a little boy, with shoes on the wrong feet, who "din know it been rainin."

You carry me on your shoulders through Wick Park, buzzing locust under foot. You baby-sit us with Bill Cosby records, with silliness and gibberish. You teach us the Funky Chicken to Sly and the Family Stone.

You are in the Navy. You answer my letters, writing "Shiver me timbers, I sure miss you, little one!"

You are home from New York, where travel becomes your passion and profession, You regale us with tales of Richard Pryor, your first big client.

You are home from LA. You bring me Rand, who will become a most treasured friend, next to you.

You take Gina and me to Spago, where we laugh at Joan Collins and George Hamilton, while eating duck pizza and drinking Moet et Chandon.

You and Rand skip arm in arm down Madison Avenue, while Kay and I huddle in her fur against the freezing cold. We go to Monkey Bar and the Four Seasons, where we laugh and drink and eat and laugh and drink. We always laugh.

You're in my kitchen. You hold my hand and talk of your mom, who lies in a bed at the Cleveland Clinic. You eat chicken and kibbee, and then nap on my couch. You give me your journal to read.

You're at Asia de Cuba, ordering "sticky rice with sticky sauce." We go to Sky Bar, and celebrate my engagement with champagne and martinis.

You're dancing at my wedding, playing derbukke with my dad, doing the dubke with my mom. Your joie de vivre shines right through your suit.

We are texting over LeBron and Kobe. I meet Shaq and send you pictures. You ask me to find out who handles his travel.

We eat at the Ivy, at Ago, the Bistro Gardens amid actors and rock stars, the beautiful and sculpted.

You are in Italy, discovering your roots; in Africa learning just who you are; in Cannes in the middle and the thick of film and art and people and food; in Russia, where they don't understand what "on the rocks" means.

Where are you Gie, Gary, Gink?

What adventure tempted you this time?

Or was it a charade, an act, a ruse?

## BLONDE AND SWEET

I conjure you
The one that I knew – the giggling girl
Blonde and sweet, like Daddy's coffee
The brown eyed girl
A prankster, a teen
Before you'd gone schooling, or sailing, or sick
Or kissed the boy with the kissing disease
Breathed in the elements, the Pacific poison
I wish we had stopped you
Not let you go
Halt, Achtung, fermere, no mas
But you were a freight train
Downwind and greased rails
The Navy, the ocean, Korea, the world
You had to live it, breathe it, to see
The air and the metal and whatever it was
That mixed with your you
And made you like that
Angry and hitting and cussing and mean
A sailor's sailor, tattoos and all
I wish you still giggled and danced on point
The ballerina beautiful
Twirling and jetting the sugarplum stage
Instead a tumor, malice itself
Spread through your brain
Seeped into your eyes
So all that you saw was colored with hate
A listless snake coiled in shade
Yanked from its torpor
Wanted revenge

Your organs folded
Like lawn chairs come fall
Wizened and withered
The you that we knew
Surfaced at last
But not fast enough
In time for hospice, forgiveness
I'm sorrys
I love yous
Denying that death
Had come to whisk you
Off to the other side

## I'M AFRAID

Yesterday, Park Vista was a rehab facility. Today it was hospice. Same building, same room, same bed. Totally different Mama.

The moment the elevator doors opened, I could hear her — A tiny flash, not a yell and not a scream. Every few seconds.

Daddy sat at her bedside, his head in his hands. Mom's eyes were open, but as far as I could tell, she could only see what was in her mind.

*How long has she been like this?*

*All day.*

We tried desperately to calm her, sooth her. Reason with her. Scold her into stopping. But she didn't. She couldn't. She just kept ahh!-ing.

A nurse was standing at the med cart just outside her door. This was unbelievable.

*Don't you hear her?*

*Oh, they get that way sometimes.*

She might as well have told me that the sink was clogged.

*Are you going to give her something or are you going to just let her suffer like this?*

*Well, there's no order from the doctor.*

*Then I suggest you pick up the phone, call a doctor, and get one. This is hospice, isn't it?*

If mother hadn't been dying, and I wasn't trying not to turn into Shirley MacLaine in *Terms of Endearment*, I would have known the names of the drugs: Haldol, Ativan. But in that moment, all I could do was keep myself from choking this woman for being so overwhelmingly indifferent.

Two weeks prior, Mom was still awake. Sepsis and white blood cells weren't yet doing their Pac Man imitation, consuming all of my mom's red blood cells. Everyone was telling her she could go home soon, and that they'd resume chemo, and that Dad would sleep on the couch next to her hospital bed with a Port-a-potty in her makeshift bedroom in the living room.

Then they stopped. We stopped.

She was still lucid, if disoriented, but mid-conversation, she'd stop, as if it just occurred to her, and say, I'm afraid.

*Oh, Mom, don't be afraid.*

I'd take her hand or Dad would sit on the bed and hold her.

*I'm afraid.*

*What are you afraid of?*

*I'm afraid.*

It was a loop that played over and over. Months before, before things were really bad, she told me, *I don't think I'm going to beat it this time.* She said she had a bad feeling. Hard as it was, I encouraged her to talk.

*I'm afraid it will hurt. That it will feel like I'm suffocating or drowning, you know, when it happens.*

I tried to assuage her fears, but I couldn't say that it wouldn't feel like that. As she got sicker, she became combative.

She scratched and batted at the nurses. She stayed awake all night and slept only if Dad or I or one of our family were there.

Eating was out of the question. Everything on her tray, including bread, was pureed and thickener was added to her water, juice, or coffee, which in and of itself was disgusting, but that had nothing to do with why she clamped her mouth closed and bit me with force I didn't know she still had.

*Don't let them give me that! They're trying to kill me. She shoved me away.*

*I'm afraid. I'm afraid. I'm afraid. I'm afraid.*

*Me? Mama, don't be afraid of me. I would never hurt you.*

Normally, when I stood to leave, her face would fall. *Do you have to go?*
Her eyes would well. I'd beg her not to cry because if she did, I'd shatter.

*Just stay ten more minutes.*

I'd sit back down, or if she wasn't really very unwell, I'd pretend like I was going to sit in her lap. Anything to make her laugh, but when I had to finally leave, she'd say, *Well, if you can hold it in, I can hold it in.* Our mutual pact not to cry. I kissed her forehead, her hands, her cheeks – one on each and a third for luck – the Lebanese way. It always made her chuckle, that I used such an old-country tradition.

But that week, she wasn't having it.

*You have to get me out of here. You're letting them kill me!*

*No, Mama. No one is trying to kill you. That's the medicine you always take.*

*Where's Albert? Albert will help me if you won't.*

Predeath agitation.

Today, when I was driving to work – because that's when the bad memories chase me – it occurred to me that it wasn't just predeath agitation or predeath delusions or predeath anything other than predeath. When everyone stopped talking about the future, about *when we get you home*, she realized that treatment was stopping so that death could start.

Giving her morphine to help with pain she did not have.

She begged for Albert – her oldest, her big strong boy, because even though he was middle aged, he was still the big, strong boy who should have been a linebacker. He could pick her up and carry her home.

It wasn't until she stopped screaming that it became real. Mama was dying. Why was this an epiphany?

Now it was my turn to plead for ten more minutes.

I'd give anything for Mama who was irritable from chemo and complained about Dad dripping coffee all over her Oriental rugs. For Mama who never liked my hair in my eyes and got upset when I used a bread knife to cut meat. Mama who told me I wore too much black and shouldn't put tomato paste in my grape leaves. Mama who a few weeks before, would pull back the covers so that I could crawl into bed with her to watch tv and eat popcorn and talk smack about people who were annoying.

Any version at all of her was better than losing her.

Ten more minutes, Mama. Just ten more.

## HOW CAN YOU TELL

Breaths short and shallow
Placid, eyelids fluttered
Waiting for a wink
A nod, a something
Untethered from rails
You no longer fought

I searched your face
Lackluster and gray
Hastily shaven by a stranger doing her job
Strips of stubble
Grown into brush escaped the mower
And false tenderness

With oiled palms
I fed your skin
Your face parched and ashen
Mmmmm you hummed
As cracks disappeared
And lines became smooth
Your eyebrows rose
Tugging at hope
That this wasn't the end

They made me starve you
Said it was kinder
He can't digest
He could drown
You have to let go

But I know what I know
And I heard relief
When I fed your face

# THE PURGE

He was here and then he wasn't
That's how it is with death
No wading in slowly
Arms aloft as you enter the cold
There's just the snap or the thud then the call
Depends how you learn
He's gone, just gone
Then there's the stuff
The callers, the meals, the handshakes and hugs
Offers, "whatever you need"
When how can you possibly know
Then there's the stuff
The actual stuff
The clothes, the shoes, copper kitchen cannisters
Sunday palms twisted into a cross
Business cards, prayer book,
A grocery list, rosary beads
A company coat with his name stitched in black
The things that say I was here
I was here
I did this stuff and that's how I lived
How do you sort what to keep, what to pitch?
How do you purge what made him him
And live with yourself for erasing
All that he was and all that he did
Whose albums you played
Sweaters you borrowed then
Snuck back in place
Whose room was cool with posters, lighters, incense, and smokes
No clock to say bedtime is now
So the scrap of paper, with bank balance, a phone number
In script, in his hand
That you know so well
Will you remember in a few years

How his t's weren't crossed
Or his A's looked like O's
If you don't see them again?
Can you preserve his smell just in your head
Or is it off to Goodwill
With all that is left
Where joking and laughing once had a home

# WHERE IS HOME

With the loveseat and couch
Where I took naps
I could finally relax
Where we had holidays
With all Mom's finery

Where is home
Where we drank coffee
From mismatched mugs
I had my favorite, from who knows where
And you mixed highballs
For us at five
Cousins stopped by
Anytime, all the time
To eat and drink
To share in your light
Where I lived that life
That got buried with you

Where is home
With my twin bed and dresser
And boots bought in high school
That never fit right
Posters of rock stars
And coats cast aside

Our things, our life, our home, our family
Scattered about
Stale bread for the birds

Where is my stuff
Like notebooks and photos
My first teddy bear
College term papers
That made mom proud

Where did it go
That home that was us
Is that still our home
Now that others live there

What is home
If I can't go visit
Where we were loud and silly and fighting and close
There's no memory farm
For me to till soil
And grow it all back

# GOOD NIGHT, YA BA

A trip to Handel's, Webb's, DQ
Windows down
We slurped
Butter pecan, chocolate black cherry

You told me stories
Of Fluke, Chink, Elmo, and Hap
At the Elm's Ballroom
With Betty and Angie
Waiting their turn
For a spin or a swing
With the jitterbug king

Then later with mom
A wink turned promise
I'll take you home for my mother to meet
You sold shoes, pizza, carpet, clothes
Anything at all to give her a home
Sapphires and diamonds
Come birthdays and such
Splurges that scared her
We can't afford this

We relived the conventions
Your only recess
From kids and work and siblings who fought
Worlds away from banal, mundane
Baloney and chips, Arak and Stoli
With the guys until dawn
When Baluga and Bellini
Could have been de rigueur
You all came from nothing
Creating a shrine
To cure sick kids in the dawn of life

We watched college ball, golf, and news
NCIS over and over
I'd lie on the couch
Just to be near you
Your everyday sayings
Reassuring not rote
You make it, I'll eat it
You wants I should help
Whaddyou doin down 'nere, said just like Jid

Always a night owl
You stayed up late
I wish I'd drunk coffee
Propped toothpicks in my eyes
But I couldn't imagine
That this was a gift
Fleeting, fading

Yawning, I'd say
I think I'll turn in
I'd bend for a hug
A kiss on each cheek
From you to me and me to you
Goodniiighttt, ya Ba
You dragged out the vowels
Softened your T
Affected Jid's accent
To make it longer
To make it last

## DO OVER

If I had a do over
I'd rub your back
Give you coffee
Black and hot, rife with caffeine
I'd give you choices
You asked me to make
I'd lie by your side
As I told you the truth
Instead of lies of omission
That fed you fear

If I had ten more minutes
I'd drink in your scent
Listen to the memories that lined your face
And quelled the fear
That spoke from your eyes
I'd hold your hand, purple with jabs
And memorize your face
Saying sorry for eye rolls
Quips meant to hurt
Hurled from my youth
To remind me today
With harrowing shame

I'd hand you a list
A thousand questions
I'd savor your voice
Your dismissive shrug
There's no time to answer
The clock's running out

But this time you'll know
That I wanted to know
If I had a do over
I think I would pass
Goodbye is too hard
Letting go, too tough
I'll take a pass
See you next time
Meet you on the other side
Where everyone is young
And we're not afraid